HOMEWARD

POEMS

RED SHUTTLEWORTH

BLUE HORSE PRESS REDONDO BEACH, CALIFORNIA 2018

HOMEWARD

RED SHUTTLEWORTH

Blue Horse Press
P.O. Box 7000 - 760
Redondo Beach,
California   90277

Cover art: "Palisades, Washington"
by Red Shuttleworth (2018).
Back cover photo
by Steve Rimple

Special thanks to Pat Murkland

Editors: Jeffrey and Tobi Alfier
Blue Horse Press logo: Amy Lynn Hayes

ISBN   978-0692143926

FIRST EDITION © 2018

This and other Blue Horse Press Titles may be found at www.bluehorsepress.com

Acknowledgments:

A number of poems in this collection received first publication in the following journals:

Chum: "In Deep Bourbon Cover"

The Cape Rock: "Hurrying into the Horizon"

Clare: "Gift-Wrapped Moses Lake"

The Laurel Review: "Rock Creek Station"

Minnetonka Review: "Great Basin Back 'n Forth"

Plains Song Review: "For Fun, You Kids Go Stand in a Dust Devil" and "Concluding Winter"

San Pedro River Review: "Filling Station Music" and "Anno Domini"

South Dakota Review: "Riderless Horses"

Suisun Valley Review: "Frontage Road... Bars... Cafes"

A number of the poems in this collection appeared in Bunchgrass Press chapbooks.

Many thanks to Jeff and Tobi Alfier (*San Pedro River Review* and Blue Horse Press) for being ever kind and generous, for publishing two previous poetry collections... and now this one.

The *Americana West* prose poem monologues were written thanks to a 2017 Tanne Foundation Award.

For

Reeser, Maggie, Bridget,

and

Patrick

Contents

"I thought then if I might travel
deep enough I might embrace
the dead as equals."

Jim Harrison
Suite to Fathers

"As the actual lived lives of most Americans become
ever more complex and fractured and, in a sense,
more generic and impersonal, we yearn for *authentic*
experiences, if only in fantasy. The West still beckons
seductively as our region of myth and the testing
ground of what remains of the American spirit."

Joyce Carol Oates
Wearing Out the West

"It is possible to be grateful that no one
that you would willingly associate with
would say, 'Be mature. Be well-balanced,
be well-adjusted.' "

Ernest Hemingway
True at First Light

Baby's Beside Me in a Fuchsia-Electric Bikini

Road-addict white tail deer…
coffee-jangled tornado-chase junkies
bullshitting each other at a cafe.
Gaunt, Route 270 is full-tilt wailin'.

Whiff of baby's strawberry-scented skin.
We're on a washboarded dusty road
close to where Gray, Oklahoma, is…
or used to be. The storm sky
has cleared to aluminum-blue.
John Conlee's on the radio,
I'm on the back side of thirty….

Soon we run out of Oklahoma
Panhandle to crazy-drive,
swerve into a Texas motel parking lot…
a few crimp-faced geezers
in overstated Waylon-style
gambler hats, mail-order frock coats.
One old man is selling framed sepia
photos of 1930's tarpaper shacks.

Outside our motel window,
a trailered Angus bull shifts weight,
groans like a mentally crippled
PE teacher out of chewing gum.
Then… baby's beside me,
sweaty in a road trip bikini,
ballet-muscled, smirking,
Care to share… a shower?

Rock Creek Station

Rangers sweep the path around
the Pony Express Station. This is where
Wild Bill hacked McCanless in front
of a young son, dispatched the boy back
to momma to say Wild Bill wanted the IOU
paid presently. No blood's left
on the ground. They broom it anyway.

Home, I go inside for jugs of sweet
strawberry Kool-Aid. We roust the girls
from the house to walk the Wolfhounds
along the creek. Kate takes off her
chopped-sleeves cowgirl shirt,
splashes hydrant water across herself.
Gazing at clouds that seem raked,
we know joy, blessed with coyote-lean
bodies to love each other with.

At loose ends at Rock Creek Station,
short of dog ownership and not quite the cook,
Wild Bill did chores for widow women.
Huddled in October Nebraska rain,
he dreamed the swell laugh of a Deadwood girl.
But there were lice to cope with,
card tricks to fathom, a ghost to create.

I went by Fairbury's Capri Motel,
where Hemingway supposedly drank one night.
Scholars have poked the walls and pulled up
floorboards in search of Cuban rum bottles.
The clerk always gives me the corporate rate.

I have carved "Camus" behind the headboard.
They once had Papa's framed photo in the office,
but a Yale kid drunkenly flung it into the pool.

At home Kate carries paper sacks
to the burning barrel. Winter is a squirrel
season away. The older hound watches
the young one paw at a possum.
Kate's face is sunburned. I come up behind
and nuzzle her coarse, long, dark hair,
and she names me the poet of sweet 'n sour
rabbit stew. I load the shotgun…
take a hike to locate dinner.

Half an Indian skeleton has been plowed up
near Rock Creek Station. Another of Wild
Bill's murders? The county sheriff
won't let the farmer get back to work
until some guys from Lincoln posse in.
Coyotes must've dined on the best parts.
Who can blame them, really?

The county sheriff denies that the scholars
are driving in their own special kind
of straw to stuff the Indian skeleton.
Wild Bill did not eat salad, I tell Kate.
Fries, on the other hand, he might've.
Watching sunrise at Gil Jackson's farm,
we try to picture a Pony Express rider
coming in for hot cocoa, showing up ready
to slaughter a few hundred chickens.
Gil asks if I really refused the salad
last night… on Western grounds.

As we're going to bed for the night,
I tell Kate that Elvis, Wild Bill, Hank Jr.,
and Hemingway all bought guns in Fairbury.
It's not about sure-fact. I slowly caress
berry-stained breasts, quietly pull back
the torn and stitched bedspread.
Blown away by two tape players
giving us versions of *Faded Love*,
I tell Kate we should try to make
a son at Rock Creek Station.

Hurrying into the Horizon

The three-night party,
all those barefoot people,
some half dressed,
and we vibrated
and the sun did not
come up for three days.

Roundup was through.
Who would eat so much
steroidal beef?
You said, *Never mind, honey.*
We went to a barn dance…
lame eighties music for Omaha friends.

We slipped away sleepy,
tucked in the kids,
sat on the front porch
with iced bottles of beer.
The full moon had not
gone down in days.

We shucked our best jeans
and snap shirts, weighted them
with boots on a mowed patch
of grass and weeds.
We stepped into our new
stock tank naked
and the moon became orange,
then the color of old corral boards.

For Fun, You Kids Go Stand in a Dust Devil

Sodbusters buried in cotton shrouds after failing
to dig-in where it was twenty moonless, black miles
to villages where quickened hearts built schools.
It is head-snapping to roam the High Plains,
to ask inelegantly, *What is so seductive*
about this country, so lovely and lonesome
under wolf-stars that pioneers stayed
as long as they could, even when down
to gnawing, sucking rat bones?

Milk cow carcasses, clouts of dry lightning,
busted scythes, gnarled nine-year-old kids
with ringworm, dogs gone hydrophobic.
It was a denim and drought shebang.

Wayne County, Nebraska, 1987

Kids in Mexican leather chaps
are clomping door-to-door in Wayne…
an icy Halloween.

We find the right field: right here
Frank and Jesse paused-bloody on their ride
from botched Northfield.

Endless ice drizzle.
Frank looks at the rich clay soil,
says, *Might pack some dirt into my wallet…*
something to save… if saving has a point.

Even with the heater full blast,
Jim's Jeep keeps Coors cold.

Abandoned farmhouses…
herbicided wells… amber moon.

Concluding Winter

The boy watches the men
near the warped-boards corral
sharpen knives, dip snuff,
judge girlfriend snapshots.
The wintered bulls are trailered,
except for a cancer-eyed Hereford.

The men's coats and jackets
are draped on corral posts
and a light south wind ruffles
them toward the Dakotas.
The boy owns two words,
Yep and *Nope*. He rides sheep
to prepare for broncs and bulls.
He wears a handed-down Resistol
battered by work and weather.

One man notes the promise of a spring
of slush and mud. The others nod, spit tobacco juice,
and a burly one joshes about a girl gone-to-town.

The men agree... sooner or later everyone
bleeds: thumbs lost to rope-crush saddlehorns,
driving on Kessler Whiskey to the tune
of lost-woman,
prom night fights... *And do you remember
that Keya Paha kid who got the earring ripped off?*

The boy watches the men stand, stretch,
and shake their heads at the bull...
good for one season,
now bound for hotdogville.

Filling Station Music

Much later in North Platte,
uncertain with a stack
of postcards: flame sky…
dazed Black Angus bull,

turn signals burned-out.

Lonesome November:
a shopping cart jammed
with cheapest beer,
a roadside punctured tire…

'n you're coughing
for someone
you mean to call
fairly soon.

The motel indoor pool:
heavy dose of chlorine…
a coffee table book on Apaches…
out in the parking lot
a misfired sawed-off .410
just for good luck.

Americana West 1906: Branchville, Texas

(Pulling a bale of hay from a short stack, Winfield, vigorous and 20, turns and notices someone. He is in rough-use farm clothes.)

There's weather and then there's weather... like there's girls and there's other kinds of girls.

Just learnt of that San Francisco earthquake. Thousands dead. Arms sticking up out of brick rubble. Blood. Bad water. More than thousands are burned out of their homes.

Let's say that an earthquake is weather. Let's call it "God's weather." You have to ask, "What is it that San Franciscans did to perturb God?" God's weather is an earthquake? I don't true-know for certain, but it's an idea.

Maybe God has a sense of humor... a humor we might take for cruel. Like there's a divine game of musical chairs that we're all playing in. The music plays and we circle a line of chairs that is one chair short for the number of people playing. So the music stops and there's someone left without a chair... a loser in God's game of chance. Now that loser is standing by himself, no food or water, but no one else is alarmed, 'cause they all got water and lamb chops on their chairs. But then the music starts up and once again everyone has to walk around the line of chairs, but one of the chairs is taken away. God's game of musical chairs proceeds... each time fewer winners. At the end, there's but one chair left, and God has placed a large sweet cake on that chair… and one fellow is the winner of that chair and that rich cake. Here's where the fun starts. The cake's too sweet and no winner can eat it all, or even eat half, and if someone tries to eat the winnings, he vomits and spoils his victory… and the rest of us, plus God, are there to laugh at the winner. Or the winner hoards the better part of his sweet, sweet cake, and then grows suspicious of everyone wanting his cake. The people in the middle… well, they get to have their cake and eat it, too. And God? He's laughing us away… all the way to Hell for most of us.

I spent a year matriculating at Baylor. Baptist school. And I'm Baptist. Don't drink. Don't dance. Don't take the Lord's name in vain.

But every so often, something riles me. So I cuss. Then I feel bad about cussin', so I take a drink to forget the sadness.

I don't dance. Except I spotted this Caldwell girl, Frances… Frances Eula. And I saw her at a picnic.

And I might want to dance with Frances Eula.

Weather.

My father farms. And I work for him. Best to get cut hay up before it rains. We mostly have cotton, but we have hay, too. And I'm talking hay.

Mostly I'm talkin' weather.

How San Francisco had its earthquake.

And us, us in Branchville, in Milam County, in by-God Texas… us… the other night we had us a thunderstorm. God's thunder. Lightning.

It blew so hard – straight line winds… or tornado – that it blew the midnight train right off the tracks. Wind derailment. People tossed around in their sleep. They'd been lulled to sleep by the train, clickety-clack of the rails. Lulled. Asleep. All of a sudden, wind, or a tornado, throws the train off the tracks. Broke arms, broke legs, one fellow with a broke spine… screaming for Jesus.

What did those passengers ever do to anger God? And the trees… pulled from the ground… flying pines. Pine trees like spears in a poem by Homer.

Don't know how much to bless and how much to curse these days. Course, my generation has it easier. I am but twenty years old. It was my grandfather and grandmother, back in the 1850's, who came to Texas. Part of a migration from Tennessee 'n Alabama.

Bless or curse?

At least the Comanche are through… finished, with no more of their raids, stealing, kidnapping our young 'uns. Comanche are gone… killed or just somewhere else.

We're here, people like me… we're here with our dreams… and our nightmares… with musical chairs for God's amusement.

Not sure how much to bless 'n how much to curse. Maybe we're blessed… and a curse is coming.

In Deep Bourbon Cover

No one wants to be
tracked down like 35-pounds
of rabid coyote.

I want something luminous-blue...
magical moon or plaid snap shirt,
Bowie knife or edgy horse.

I kick into oblivion hotels,
strapped to jet-black
notebooks of frosty hindsight.

Locate me at the edge
of a West where no revelation lasts
longer than Great Basin rainwater.

Casino Oatmeal

A platoon of old guys sits the cafe counter
in Stockman's as I stagger-in
for a chicken fried steak
and fried eggs ten a.m. breakfast.
A couple of geezers look over, so I nod,
and their eyes glint, *You're gonna be*
sittin' with us in ten years… if you don't
heart attack out, you dumb bastard.

The waitress, peroxide-blonde okay at forty,
says, *It'll be just a little while, honey.*
The closest geezer spoons
buttery raspberry oatmeal.
Most have Resistols or Stetsons
screwed down on their skulls…
sweat-stained, short-brimmed grandpa hats.

I think about my daughters…
when they had ragdolls,
Barbies, tea parties
with Wolfhounds.
And I think back to when
my son rode dry ewes,
spurred straw and alfalfa bales
with growl 'n roughstock hooks.

I think about the blind miles
on poetry road: cold eyes,
lipsticked bubble lips,
the ruined figures of lady
freshman composition teachers,
motels with not-so-anonymous

coed door knocks after readings,
all the brain-bruise wake-ups,
and the rush to the car
to speed down-road.

And I think of poets onward
and away from poetry…
now making stained glass
or selling hedge funds,
paying bad-house mortgages,
their kids breaking knick-knacks
with hurled skateboards.

Now the old guys
are weaving out of Stockman's,
so I nod again and they nod,
their eyes flashing,
You're gonna get yours…
sure as ugly weather,
sure as BLM stealin' grazing land,
sure as wives pushing vitamin pills,
hip replacement, pointless drives
to Mexico for prostate cancer cures.

This Was Once Wild Horse Country

A few miles southwest of Sparks,
half-poised homecoming queen candidates
strut a stage in sleek pink dresses.
Mangy skateboarders, eye-pop-eager
on momma's pills, leave chicken blood
on the front steps of a high school.
The girl most favored to be queen
giggles on bargain vodka,
swallows tobacco juice.

Out on the desert near Gerlach,
Burning Man clean-up crew gone,
autograph seekers with nylon string guitars
pester a Marilyn Monroe impersonator
swathed in a dusty black cotton sheet.
Marilyn is chloral-dancing alone
for Clark Gable's ghost.

Great Basin Back 'n Forth

Is it forbidden to say,
She's knocked-up?
Guileless, the children
of the one-room knobby school
sing, *You must allow for the bond*
For she's a pretty fucky blonde.

~

And tonight no one
minds the grocery store
as children pick
the back door lock:
Gummy Worms...
creaky hinges to the upstairs
room where unbidden
kisses are received.

~

The preacher says,
The nails from Christ's cross
burn acid-hot in our hearts.
And the slim first row boy
blushes at the girl
across the purple aisle
for one more sweet dose
of psychobilly love.

The Heart Gnaws on Itself

No more bed-bounce
love storms. Dead town.
Lost prom tickets,
dried 'n rustlin' rabbit brush,
a hammock with a hole,
birth certificate ashes
softly blow across the floor
of the train station.
The sun flashes
off a couple of rusted clouds.

Old Silver... Aged Stars over Nevada... the Usual Bluff

A little money, half a continent to drift,
you're a past-peak gunslick of the non-rhyme.
Today you're driving 35 or 95, nothing average,
seeking badger-silence, the next cinderblock motel.

Stars overhead with ragged postage stamp edges:
glitter for the begging. The sleek Chinese girl
at Mona's Ranch refuses to believe you're only there
for a T-shirt. She wants to camisole-strip real slow.

Legends have their own cares. Doc Holliday coughs
at the underside of a Glenwood Springs gravestone.
And Jesus fondle's Mary M.'s breasts, pounds a jug
off a table in Heaven to scare off missionaries.

And... when you flip on the motel bathroom light,
it flashes before dying. With whiskey head-throb,
with strawberry-taste skin-memories of someone,
it's good to sleep with a .45 below your pillow.

Ghost Town Hotel

A raw button-down sky,
your sweet marzipan kisses,
a bonfire as mirror:
whiskey-'n-love blistered
at Great Basin dawn.
We sleep on mustang bones.

Moonless Great Basin Mad-Night

Ranchers at the counter in Stockman's...
checking the dates on nickels.

~

Gnashed teeth in a low-down Ely motel room.

~

The dreams of mice in fresh open graves.

~

The odor of music as cassette tapes burn.

~

Radioactive Nevada dirt under the fingernails.

~

Forty-first Vegas no-rain night. Forty-two nights
past the casino parking lot drowning of a tourist.

Americana West 1911: Sidney, Montana

(*A hump of ground on a rutted, muddy, slushy road bordered by a three-strand barb wire fence. Jincy, maybe 15, crawls… swims mud to the hump… makes claim to it. Jincy is in a cloth coat, men's trousers, a scarf around her neck… lathered, caked with mud.*)

Clank of pot on pan. Bang of pan on pot. Jounce 'n jolt me. Me? I am Jincy. Jincy. And it all falls from the wagon. Sleet. Rainy snow for hours. We pulled from Sidney in sleet.

My name is Jincy. What custom of name do I have? Jincy?

Jincy is what Minnesota nuns said I was. Jincy. A spawn of sinners. Orphan. An orphan among other orphans, but then a girl-orphan turned young bleeder… and the priests… the priest who could see in the dark… who could see darkness. Jincy darkness.

The nuns sold me… to be a house girl. Servant girl. Sold to the Nabletts. Mr. and Mrs. Nablett. They came to St. Joseph's Home for Children. The Nabletts… at the orphanage they redeemed me.

I was bought. With coin. Judas coin.

Last night… in Sidney. The Nabletts camped in a livery stable. I was left with the wagon. To sleep under the wagon.

Much to be learned under a wagon... next to a stable.
From the talk. From listening....

What I learned:
It is near Christmas.
This is a flood plain.
The Missouri River is just north.
This place... it does flood.

Oh... to be Jincy. Before Jincy I was.... I do not
proper know. Monica? Abby? Is there blessing in the
name Jincy? Or is it mud from sleet... the slip-sound
of wagon wheel?

Here I am... on the road west from Sidney. On this
hump of ground... protrusion of road. Rutted track.
Slushy. A road with ice ponds.

It is nineteen and eleven. I was born in another
century. I am fifteen. To be a house girl for the
Nabletts... bound for Jordan... to be merchants.

The Nabletts tied bundles, pots and pans... tied them
to the wagon. And I was lashed with cord, tied with
old cord... twine and wire... tied to the wagon, too. I
clattered with pans. And I dropped into sleep. And I
dropped off the wagon. No one looked back.

Crack-of-tooth cold. Soon worse. How worse?
Crack-of-bone cold. That worse. Then... shake-'n-
soil-self cold.

Such wind… wet snow. Such weather noise. The
Nabletts failed to hear clatter of pot and pan and me,
Jincy… failed to hear us fall to the road.

I swam and crawled… dog paddle and crawl. To
here… to this place. Dream a foundling redeemed. A
birth in snowy mud. Alone… ice rain and sleet.
Orphan-lost. Slowly… darkness overtakes the
world… like a trousers-down priest at night.

Here is my place? This upturn of ground… on a
rutted road of no traffic? On-the-crawl… at-swim
across high plains. Alone with wind-howl. December
howl.

(*She gets to all-fours and wolf-howls.*) Conjure… a high
plains December death-dream! (*She wolf-howls again.*)

Flood-Scarred Early Summer

A 19th century nickel-plated pistol
might be worth more than a volunteer
flood lake over a section of winter wheat.

A sinewy woman in a Liberty County,
Montana, grocery store, asks if she
might put milk and cornflakes on the tab.

New Mexico burns… Montana backstrokes
swollen rivers. An old rancher folds
a newspaper, hides the weather report.

Over a hundred cow-calf pairs
sold to make it through, a rancher
drags a recliner into an empty corral.

A drifter buys a black bread sandwich,
roast beef on wilted lettuce, in Rudyard,
saddle blankets dirt-cheap at a lawn sale.

Railroad Tracks Across the Milky Way

Don't worry about what that fragrance is
as you hike the lung-shaped canyon.

Someone says, *Tell me, lover, please tell me.*
And someone grumbles, *Let me go*, but hangs around.

You gaze through mirrors and glass... so high
into a rocket-punched sky... to where it is icy-black.

A two-year-old girl squeezes her father's hand,
Look! The moon is going to the grocery store!

You dizzy-dance alone on a rough hardwood floor.
A crepe-festooned coyote appears at a window.

Frontage Road... Bars... Cafes

I walk slow from my orange-carpet motel room
to the nearest cafe. The music is not
Townes Van Zandt,
and it ought to be, but I sit for chicken fried steak,
green beans, marionberry pie, iced tea.
It's just another lonesome eyes highway.

God's cunning, some guy says to me, unable
to order a Diet Snapple with whiskey.
He's about ready to tilt over into my booth.
So I tell him, *There's absolutely no reason
for us to know each other*, because I realize
he said, <u>*coming*</u>, not <u>*cunning*</u>.

Outside there's a splash of green
in a storm-pewter sky and it's starting
to hail marbles onto cars, loud
as a knock-kneed whore on cheap blow.

Fayette, North Dakota, 1926

From dry hills, the lands looks like fire-yellow stone.
The wind purrs across ragged silence.
A boy sits home with his grandmother.
She has pneumonia, clucks at jokes.
Her skin is the color of a baked potato.
What's left is the humdrum of dying.
Grandma once lived on a dancehall street,
a crafty isolate sewing plush grizzly bear dolls.
The boy makes hand shadows on the wall.
Grandma tells about the gutted corpse
found in a Chinese laundry's hamper,
how the sheriff sat beside a dead man…
ate a supper of pork chops, apple sauce, whiskey.
The grandmother was born in Indiana,
nearby mules chewing corn,
the murky day the Civil War commenced.
Impervious to the boy's fiddle tune,
grandma's eyes bulge as she crawls off the bunk.

Mule-Eared, Knee-High Boots

Icy coyote pack in dawn light.
Happiness plums... next dessert.

Ashes Canyon after many funerals:
sluggish noon rattler and a gold clasp.
High-pitched coyote yips and barks.

Autumn rain on a sun-faded farmyard sofa.
She asks, *Are you quite sure?*

The down-leg slide of her linen skirt...
colors of last July's wheat harvest.
Roses... rain-soaked boots.

The Masks of Love

From Luke Shuttleworth

Cowboy heuristics:
The woman you're dating
is younger
than the music
you're listening to.

The Taking Up

Ratshot .22, fired from six yards....
No rattler penetration from a wide-pellet pattern.

Town lights south of the freeway,
a sand-yellow sky,
go-for-broke flapjacks
with butter, quarters of orange.

Later: desperate freestyle swimming...
at five miles an hour
in your own pulmonary artery,
you are faint... unclear.

Time... Phantoms

First yellowed poplar leaves...
rattler to a den.

Cottontail scream and a red sunset.
A split-lipped coyote corners

toward the moon as it rises
through wildfire smoke.

Americana West 1925: Quartzburg, Idaho

*(A deadfall bar, sawdust floor, pine planks across greasy,
grimy wood barrels. Finbar turns around from the bar,
schooner of watery beer in one hand. Finbar, 55 or older, is
in a distressed white shirt, vest, solid-gray necktie, dark
trousers, and miner boots.)*

Forget about... Calvin Coolidge.

Forget about... *The Great Gatsby*.

Forget about... Darwin's Monkey Theory.

These are passing phenomenon. Let them pass like
the anus-gas that they are.

*(Finbar drinks the rest of his beer, sets down the glass
schooner. He produces a tin whistle, performs a small jig as
if to loosen up a bit... and he plays a snatch of an old tune.)*

I'll tell you of an immortal event.

In 1909, in San Francisco, your man here, meself,
Finbar... Finbar from St. Clement's Road in Dublin...
in 1909 I served as cornerman for the great
Middleweight Champion of the World, served as the
cornerman for Stanley "The Michigan Assassin"
Ketchel when he fought a dozen rounds... when he
fought to take away the Heaveyweight Championship
from the great Jack Johnson.

*(Finbar plays some on his tin whistle... does a pugilistic
jig.)*

Remember… Ketchel was but a middleweight…
around 155 pounds for this fight… and remember that
Jack Johnson was 200 pounds.

The deal was… for Ketchel and Johnson were
friendly… the deal was they would dance about…
give no more than a boxing exhibition. And once it
was over, the fellows were going to go visit an opium
den with some girls of the Barbary Coast.

That's what the plan was… a friendly plan.

But Ketchel, in the twelfth round, stunned Johnson,
punched him so mightily, that Johnson went down.

But Johnson sprang back up, like a great whale, came
back up… and struck Stanley Ketchel so hard with a
near-mortal punch, that Ketchel's front teeth, his
beautiful snow-white front teeth… hit him so hard
that those front teeth were embedded in Jack
Johnson's boxing glove.
(*Finbar plays a sharp note on his tin whistle for
exclamation.*)

Ketchel was knocked out for ten minutes in the ring!

For ten devilish minutes the great Stanley Ketchel was
on the canvas. Some thought Stanley was dead. We
poured water on him. A doctor gave him all manner
of stimulents: smelling salts… urine powder from
sporting girls!

For ten minutes the great Stanley Ketchel was dead-
on-his-back.

And Jack Johnson... Jack Johnson, Heavyweight
Champion of the World, slowly picked Ketchel's teeth
from his boxing glove... picked out the four white
front teeth... and flicked them onto the canvas where
Ketchel lay dead-to-the-world.

Busy as I was trying to revive Stanley... I saw the
teeth bounce on the canvas of the ring... one tooth, a
second tooth... tooth three. Tooth four.

It was meself... I was the man who collected all four
of Stanley "The Michigan Assassin" Ketchel's teeth.

(*He plays a few notes on the tin whistle.*)

Less than a year later, me friend 'n benefactor, the
great Stanley Ketchel, at a health farm, trying to get
over certain addictions, trying to get back into fighting
trim, was shot dead by a jealous common-law
husband.

It was a tragedy written by the fucking ghost of
Shakespeare.

(*Finbar plays a note or two on the whistle, sets it down,
produces a brown glass prescription bottle, which he holds
up and shakes like a rattle.*)

Gents, I have in me hand, the four front teeth of the
Great Stanley Ketchel... knocked out by the Great Jack
Johnson, Heavyweight Champion of the World.

What true man, for the sake of luck, what true man will stand me a drink to hold Ketchel's teeth in the palm of his hand?

(*Finbar opens the bottle, pours four teeth into his hand.*)

What true man will stand me a drink?

For Ketchel's teeth hold more luck than a Galway shamrock… more luck than a leprechaun's foreskin on a nun's finger.

Is there a true man who'll stand a whiskey to hold Ketchel's teeth? Good Lord. Teeth? This is a chance to hold the very *Light of the World* in your hand.

A Few Hundred Miles... Homeward

Black tears pour
down a basalt cliff.
Ache of a nameless cloud.

~

Half-memory returns
of eating goat steak.
Acres of Great Basin wind.

~

Emerald light of evening flowers
& cinnamon scent of dancers:
lonesome far away fires.

~

Kidney-jabbing road north
from Fallon... a hawk fades...
indigo dream-horses in my side mirror.

Primitive Road

Past the swirl of dull yellow graveyard dust,
shallow-root trees, homemade toys at roadside….

A farmhouse, tiny windows, gently sways
beneath oval-carved clouds.

It is so easy to end up broke… with no more
than an end-crust of pocked rye bread.

A farmer sweeps black grit off a porch bed,
sets aside his father's eagle head cane.

On a steep westward downside of a rutted two-track,
a cowboy in a careening pickup hears his heart rough-thump.

Anno Domini

1.
Autumn-suede grasslands.
A father waits-up
for his boozy son, hoping the boy won't
wreck the pickup, hurt himself or a stranger.
The man can smell tangled metal,
the burning rubber of his own youth...
blue cobalt light flooded with red flares.

2.
A black moon dances.
Lovers burn rags beside a lake.
Yesterday's snow wisps in corn stubble.
This is what yellow eyes see....
The lovers bend to the smoke,
take dry gulps of starlight.

3.
The growl the man hears is like a steel guitar
dragged behind a horse on a gravel road...
thumping walls of a honky tonk,
angels in denim 'n fleece,
blue faces in whirling light.
Blind stars blink, *Vacancy... Vacancy.*

Shower Clouds to the South

Barn owl... corncrake...
an afternoon dream.

A neighbor sells
a twenty-year-old
dapple-gray...
pipe corral ornament...
can't get the gelding trailered.
A little boy circles... shudders 'n weeps.

August corn going brown
at the edges of fields.
Lush alfalfa at another neighbor's...
soon a last good cutting.

If There Is Anything

It's a roadside flood-lake
above an ulcerated coulee's village…
Easter basket and candies
likely tossed from a car window.

Spring: stout gleam
in the eye of an Angus bull.

Wine-blue sky… sunset coming.

A line of ancient
fallen gray cedar fence posts,
wire-broke or loose beyond purpose.

Stillness and Dust

So many caught under the moon's heel...
cans of condensed milk,
voices of creek stone for memory,
easy-crack old hips 'n ribs....

For company, the rustle of moonlight vines
outside a small fallen-to-ruin brick hotel.

The hands and feet tingle.
The mirror has grown a white-bristled face.
For thirst there's a stainless steel pail
half full of cloudy sink water.

For sleep: a bygone cowboy's
ripped quilt, blood-spotted single bed.
For dreams: the sorry-soil farms
where parents shallow-buried firstborn.

Lost World of the Horse-Drawn

You see it in the eyes of mounted deer heads....

Barmaids in thin cotton gym shorts,
muted TV screens in strip mall offices,
shooting galleries of bankrupt traveling carnivals.

In the heyday, when things mattered,
stovepipe hats had arrows through them.

Shadows of a Dying Town

Old time electric chair for sale.

Sunday picture shows
whir in the storage room
of an abandoned filling station.

Cemetery stone inscription: *Bootmaker.*

Beyond the local bar,
a mile of highway
littered with lipstick-stained paper napkins.

A cow-calf pair grazes a field off Main Street.
No cafe. Just old, crumbly photos of a cafe.

At the back end of the graveyard,
a rusty shovel lost in sagebrush.

Sonnet Fragment

for Paul Zarzyski

Hazy evening... not a speck of glitter
off rattlesnake skin... plenty of cloud-
shade to honor spring's first thunderstorm.

There is this wait... locked into thirst.
Tall, deep-green lush grass...
where there isn't sagebrush.

Long back, you placed money on song...
poetry... busted corral boards, barn wood,
cracked fence posts, roll-over-you
outlaw horses... toward the only grace.

Riderless Horses

Before packing the U-Haul, there was a yard sale,
the mowing of a two-acre lawn their goats avoided,
the shooting with a .357 of three penned terrier mutts.
Then they drove away with their children,
left behind a pair of half-starved horses
for an animal rescue outfit to pick up.

It happened a few miles sunward.
An alfalfa farmer told me.
He was at our house, cutting
a crawl space hole in a closet ceiling.
We looked into the attic, joked…
hoped to find ancient photo albums,
a skeleton, a box of Bowman 1940's baseball cards.

Last night I heard riderless horses
a hundred yards away… on the gravel two-track.
The Wolfhound led me outside to stand
beneath cold solitude-stars.
Gas may be down to three bucks,
but the price of rice still leads
to shooting family dogs.

No Going Back

Abandoned horse ranch... cigarette holes
in family picture albums... the work of flashlight tourists.

Within a decade, county-wide dry wells. The moronic
junior college president poses under a center pivot.

You're chopping weeds. Eating defrosted blueberries.
You're an elderly child of a carcass-rich scabland.

The upcoming Walmart fashion season: plastic bear claw
necklaces to accessorize dog-skin jackets from China.

Nostalgia... Eureka, Nevada

A hollow-husk girl with streaky makeup
slips into Raine's Market, pauses to glare
at mounted bear, deer, bobcat heads
not too high above motor oil cans,
Hostess cherry-lard pies, Purina Puppy Chow
in small and medium sacks... a couple of rips.
She's got $2.73 and reckons it can buy
a plastic-wrapped turkey sandwich,
plus a twenty-ounce Coke, which it can't.
I drop a twenty on the counter for her grub...
say nothing when the girl keeps my change.

~

The horizon is neutral-blue, not cobalt
like I want it to be. Thanks to Wally,
my photo-poster's all over town, my face
plum-red, distorted by his ancient printer
in the Eureka Opera House.
A woman my age recognizes me,
tries to sell me a fake wolf head
set in a prayer wheel... thirty-five bucks...
and she'll toss in a soda pop for free.
I am the Great Basin's poet-on-the-road,
with a clean room at the Sundown Lodge.
The fake wolf head's glass eyes
snare me half an hour later,
so I leave my whiskey
on the bar at the Owl Club,
half-jog back to the store up the street.

~

Wally says that a skateboarder, Eureka's first,
got taken down by his ear by the woman
who sold me the fake wolf head.
Word is that the skateboarder's mom
says she is going to have someone arrested
for unnecessary roughness.
At the local museum, I buy a warped blank
greeting card so I can write all this to you.

Gift-Wrapped Moses Lake

Earlier, after the thunderstorm blew north,
a gaggle of girls, one with henna-red hair
in cornrows, were on a Walmart boyfriend hunt,
loose floral sundresses, one in tight jeans
and a brief red blouse with blue paint splotches.
The tallest girl said to the one eating chocolate,
You even fake your own thoughts.

Vietnam war vets were outside the stores,
asking for donations for red paper poppies,
distraught over lost comrades called to mind,
melancholy as threadbare slippers, yet clean-shaven
for the first time, perhaps, in a week or so.
At the post office, one veteran's grown son,
in rubber waders, licked his own forearm,
time and again, until his father walloped him.

Canned television laughter and the sound
of Kate washing dishes: this is life…
a collection of moments so ordinary with surprise,
composed of honey-colored flames and smoke.

... but wonder if...

Spring surprise on a gravel
irrigation district two-track:
some farmer tractor-dragged a dead
or dying cow to a winter-dry ditch... left it
to transmogrify to a complete, intact,
reasonably still attached
crow-pecked cow skeleton.
Curiously... no coyote-spread of bones.

Stone-gray clouds, emerald fields
of timothy and alfalfa. Such radiance!

About the Author

Red Shuttleworth is a three-time recipient of the Spur Award (from Western Writers of America) for Poetry: *Johnny Ringo* (2013), *Roadside Attractions* (2011), and *Western Settings* (2001). In 2016 he won the Western Heritage Wrangler Award for "Outstanding Poetry Book" for *Woe to the Land Shadowing*. He received a 2017 Tanne Foundation Award for Poetry and Playwriting. Shuttleworth was named "Best Living Western Poet" in 2007 by *True West* magazine. His poetry and short plays have appeared in numerous journals. His plays on the West have been presented widely.